NOTES OF AN INDIGENOUS FUTURIST

Cliff Taylor

Published in the United States by Hema Press,
an imprint of Hyeay LLC.
hemapress.com
ISBN 979-8-9907270-1-4

Printed in the United States of America
Cover design by Hema Press
Photograph on Cover by Cliff Taylor

*Both Publisher and Author would like to acknowledge Gina McWaters
for the connection-magic she made before this book was even an idea: Weblaho!

Dedicated to the Indigenous Future
flowering deep within us all.

CONTENTS

PART ONE

PART TWO

PART THREE

PART ONE

HOW I REMEMBERED THE GRASS

As a Ponca born at the end of the 20th century I was staggered and astonished by an endless number of things, but as a book lover I was just totally mystified that up until I'd published my memoir, *The Memory of Souls*, only one other single book had ever been published by a Ponca in the hundred plus years previous. One single Ponca-written-and-published book out there on the rippling ocean of modern culture, broadcasting its solitary story.

If you're not familiar with it it's titled *How I Remembered the Grass*, and it's a slim little science fiction novella about a Ponca who hides inside a buffalo's carcass when the Government comes hunting tribal members who were trying to escape relocation, and he somehow falls through a portal in the buffalo that takes him to a far off future that's actually quite beautiful where he spends the rest of his life, haunted by the slowly fading memories of his first life with his tribe in Niobrara (our tribe in Niobrara, maybe I should say).

It's a little dry, mostly forgotten, but the story between the lines was and is heart-rending to me. It was the only written account from another Ponca that existed for me when I was young and searching and trying not to let all the monsters swallow me up. I held it close like an inherited eagle feather, frayed and tattered but full of meaning.

Do you know this book?

If not, please, seek it out and read it. The soul that wafts through its pages is savagely beautiful.

STILL IN THE CAVES

I have memories from when
I was young of what I'd
heard were still in certain
hidden caves in Nebraska.

Things that'd make my
Indian soul glow with wonder
if I ever actually got to
see them with my own eyes.

I'm proud that we still have
things that haven't been handled
and studied by all the scientists
and archeologists.

Every time I drive by those caves
I think of pulling over and hiking
down into them, to behold those
sacred things I heard about
when I was young.

BROTHER JOEY

Finally having a day off, I head over to my pal Joey's house where he's living it up bachelor-style with his wife down in Florida for the month.

I knock, am let in, am mauled by their enormous dog, mosey over to the couch as Joey finishes up a rollicking call with a guy I gather is named Kosmo. I look out the window at the Megler Bridge, the peaceful (today) Columbia River, the ships passing by.

"Later, Kosmo! Yeah, my buddy's here. Yeah! Later!"

Joey, almost 60, a long-time professional musician in LA, slim, black-haired, comes over and stands like he's about to go somewhere even though he's not actually going anywhere at all.

"You know who that was?"

"Who?"

"That was Kosmo, the manager of The Clash in the 70s."

"The Clash?!"

"Yeah, The Clash. He came into some records I might be interested in."

"Damn. Cool."

When you move to a new town you never know who you're going to make friends with; I never meet any Poncas, but I do always meet some rad/good/interesting/brother-deep kindred spirits.

He looks at me with a light in his eyes that just makes me smile.

"So, what's up?"

YOU'RE NOT EVEN PRETENDING

I'm constantly imagining the poems
my descendants will write once
we've emerged from the apocalypse
of colonization and fully gotten
back on our able feet.

They'll be crafting songs and
masterworks of memory and joy,
spiritual genius and fully realized
ceremony; there won't be as
much horror and family car wrecks
as there is today, as much
hopelessness and death.

I pretend I'm collaborating with
them, trading notes and visions,
knowledge of what happened and
what's to come.

I pretend so deeply that my
ancestors begin to whisper to
me, "You're not even pretending
anymore. What you're seeing
is real."

FATHER AND SON MEMORIES

HBO played non-stop on my grandpa's big console TV when I was a little kid visiting him and all my aunts and uncles back in the day.

I sat in front of it and played with my action figures, was transfixed by what I saw, bored, scared, assaulted, tickled, taken away on so many journeys. It was like some new god that was guiding all of us beaten-up Indians through the hollow, plastic wilds of the invasive American culture.

I saw movies I shouldn't have, good ones in constant rotation that I remember to this day, Eddie Murphy, The Howling II, Conan the Barbarian. For many years I remembered a scene where these scruffy Frenchmen were swinging from chandeliers and swordfighting a roomful of bloody vampires in some castle. It was like a memory from another world. When I was in my thirties I finally stumbled across the movie it was from: *Captain Kronos: Vampire Hunter*. I bought it used for 5 bucks. It actually held up.

I watched HBO and played with my men till my barfighter dad would come into the room to take me someplace. He was strong, mean, his love hidden.

"Time to hit the road, son," he'd say.

"Let's go."

CHASING NEPHEWS

Pushing cars out of ditches
with other Indians in
a blizzard.
Riding on a Mad Max golf cart
to a sweat in Kauai with a
hippie smoking a joint.
Recounting Bigfoot stories
at the Co-op with my coworkers
and getting chills.
Chasing my nephew around
the backyard as the moon
and the stars really
begin to sparkle.
Hugging ghosts of old lost
Poncas every time they
show up on my doorstep.
Devising ways to get our LANDBACK
as we smoke cigarettes in
the cold.
Getting our aching bodies up
to dance some more when it's
time to honor our leaders.
Feeding bread heels to the ducks
with my mom when I was
a toddler.
Promising the spirits I'd tell

as many of our stories as I could
while I'm here.
Kissing my long-time partner
for the first time when we
were just falling in love
in Seattle.

PUZZLES AND PORTALS: PART ONE

I awoke in a library, in what felt like a University's less-frequented sub-basement.

How I got there I had no clue.

My shoes were on, my clothes were intact, my wallet was reassuringly in my back pocket.

The shelves were full, plain, not dusty or anything, tended even, I'd say.

It was strange but I was short on time for strangeness so I began to make my exit.

I found a stairwell, took it to the next floor and then the floor after that, and then the floor after that too.

After several floors an uneasy feeling began to lodge in my stomach: how many floors could there be and more eerily, where were any of the other people?

Hours passed and I discovered, as far as I could tell, that I was in an empty library all by myself that seemed to have no exits, no windows to the outside world, and no end to its floors and books.

But I did find some food.

At one of the study tables there was a sack lunch with a fresh sandwich, some chips, an apple, and a Pepsi, just sitting there.

I ate it, scarfed it down, and screamed.

I explored, checked the books, all of which were real but in no particular order on the shelves, ate more fresh lunches I found, and called out to no avail for anyone else who was in there.

Days passed, then weeks.

I was stuck in a puzzle that was edged with horror.

Someone or something was feeding me.

The structure of the library was well-maintained, accommodating, not too cool or not too warm, peaceful to a strong degree.

I didn't know what to do but like all people, I desired my freedom.

I found a book on Sitting Bull, read it, and kept it with me, my guardian angel warrior Chief who was going to help me escape.

"Help me, grandpa," I said, staring at his face on the cover.

"Help me to find my way out of here."

PUZZLES AND PORTALS: PART TWO

Months into my stay in the endless University library, I came across something that was both more madness and my first sign of hope: a small book on birds that, when I opened it, turned out to be a full-on portal to my reality, to my home.

I could stick my fingers through the portal and feel the air I knew with my skin.

I could peer through its tree-secured (?) vantage point and watch the woods there, occasionally even see what looked to be some hikers.

When I made the mistake of letting the book close though, it reopened as just another ordinary book.

But somehow I knew that there were other books like this one too, ones containing portals back to my world.

I ate my sack lunches and searched for them.

Quickly, I discovered that they were all hidden in books too thin for me to actually crawl through, and that they all only worked or functioned that one initial time when you opened them.

Looking constantly, I found about one per week.

I saw snow, people, jungles, kids playing video games, city councils, cows, domed cities.

I could put my fingers through, observe, and that was pretty much it.

But I believed that there had to be a portal in a book big enough for me to crawl through, so that I could get home.

I looked and looked and, honestly, maybe a year passed.

I read, ate, slept, looked at random bits of home, and searched all of the books.

It fueled me to at least be able to see my world, to see life continuing on.

And then I quit finding my portals.

Any at all.

It was just me and the library again; endless, alone, quiet, books my only companions.

I talked to my Sitting Bull book, scratched at my scraggly head, saying, "Where have my windows to home gone?

"How come I can't see our home anymore?"

PUZZLES AND PORTALS: PART THREE

Years passed.

I stayed healthy even if my clothes fell apart on me.

One time I did find one more portal book and watched a fireworks display unfold over an enormous river, people all over, but that was the last one.

One time I swear I saw someone's shadow crossing up the stairs on another floor and when I went for my sack lunch up there it was eaten up and gone.

I read to comfort myself, always looking for a good Indian book.

I danced, had nightmares, screamed.

I walked up for days, for miles.

I walked down for days, for miles.

I tried everything I could.

Decades passed.

I became old.

Even older than my companion and friend Sitting Bull, whose book I brought everywhere with me.

And then I found it: a book on Africa as big as a coffee table that was a portal when I opened it.

I held it open and looked at its empty prairie ocean for days.

Was I too old to leave now?

Did I still want to leave?

How do things like this happen to people, unexplainable, torturous, unasked for things?

Naked, I sat there and just watched.

"I get to decide where I die," I thought.

"This is still my story."

A groan moved through the whole library like a corrupt whale's grief-song, and I shuddered.

I'd never heard anything but silence and my own voice in the library itself before.

I shook my head and thought about closing the book, going to get a sack lunch.

Then I threw Sitting Bull through the portal and watched him land in the wild grass; my book, my friend, my Chief.

The groan rumbled through the library again.

Maybe someone else was beginning to wake up in the endless library.

It was time for me to go.

I heard Sitting Bull getting up, telling me, "No horror can last forever…"

The groan made me twist.

I didn't want to leave and yet all I wanted to do was leave.

The groan came again, pitiful, pained, mindless.

I took a breath, winked at Sitting Bull, and dove on through.

PUZZLES AND PORTALS: PART FOUR

This world turned out to not be my world either.

I've wandered for months seeing no life but myself.

No libraries.

No new friends.

My conversations with Sitting Bull continue, remain as alive as ever.

I'm in shreds, but I'm fine.

A strange earth shimmers all around me.

Mountains, stars, big, breathing trees, the tracks of beasts I have yet to encounter.

I'm content.

I have my health, my will.

I'm still Indian, and that has gotten me this far.

I walk, study, appreciate, ready myself, consult Chief, marvel, share breath with the world, hope, and eat the sack lunches I find.

I believe there's someone waiting for me, trusting that I'll find them.

I believe tomorrow could be the day.

Tomorrow could be the day when all of this strange misfortune finally comes to an end.

A PONCA WRITER (ME) ON NEBRASKA PUBLIC RADIO

I was on NPR for the first time today
and I couldn't believe it.
Did a flaming horse enter the coffee shop?
Did a healing rain fall down all across
Niobrara?

As far as I know, it was the first time a
Northern Ponca artist or writer of any kind
has ever been on NPR.
"Representation is so crucial, can be so
life-changing," I told the host.
"Thank you for giving me this opportunity
and for allowing me to speak about our
tribal reality on the radio.
This is going to spark things to life in
all sorts of hearts out there, in all
sorts of Ponca hearts out there."

I hung up the phone and listened to the birds
in the bushes outside my window, drank
my hot tea.

In the distance I saw my grandpa Chief Standing Bear
smiling at me, telling me with his eyes
that I'd done good.

NATIVES LOVE HORROR MOVIES, PERIOD

I need to write a long essay about
why all of us Natives love our
horror movies so much.
I mean, it should be clear:
we're all like the characters in those movies!
We're haunted, we encounter truly bloodthirsty
monsters, the supernatural is constantly in
our midst, we've known since we were born
that something very powerful has wanted us dead.
See, we relate to the stories told in the
horror movies.
But you know what else?
Most of the time the final girl slays the
slasher, the monsters are obliterated, hell
is pushed back into the puzzle box, and
good triumphs over evil-
and we relate to that key piece too-
that piece of the ending that says the good guys
were always going to win.
Yup, if you didn't know it yet, we Indigenous Peoples
are the good guys and according to the grand design
of this great holy story that Mother Earth is telling
we're going to emerge time and time again
as her best and most heroic
expressions—

it was just something She put in our contract,
in the Original Instructions she gave us.
Oh look!
Puppet Master 3 is on!
The essay and the rest of this poem will
have to wait.
The popcorn's ready and for me and my
whole rambunctious, wild-eyed Indian gang,
it's time for the show!

YOUR IMAGINATION IS
A BIGFOOT SHRINE

Our imagination is this secret book we have that the spirits are writing in and filling up as we go about our lives.

I remember this as we rumble along the farmer's road up in Santee away from our family's timeless Sundance grounds, trees marching around us, the big Nebraska sun pressing its glowing hands onto every bit of the land.

We Native people have always known that the Sacred is brilliantly alive inside of our sweet and humble human bodies, manifesting mysteriously in all sorts of ways.

I grip the steering wheel of my giant old car (remember when cars were metal and steel?) and feel home singing into me from all directions, a goodbye, a welcome back, a see you soon.

Our imagination is a part of this sacred life within; receiving impressions of what's possible, what once was, what could be, what truly is, always.

I turn out of the farmer's field and onto the reservation's quiet brown gravel road, full of love smoke, a burning appreciation for my life, and see hundreds of Bigfoot pausing in the surrounding fields to honor and acknowledge me, to wave goodbye and call out to me, to dance a little for the joy of it all in these moments we're sharing until we meet again.

I listen to my own imagination and am grateful for everything the spirits have to say.

I mean, who doesn't want to receive a farewell from the Bigfoot when they're leaving the Sundance grounds?

ANNIVERSARY IN MT. HOOD

My girlfriend and I sit on some fancy chairs at an orchard on the famous Fruit Loop around Mt. Hood in Oregon, eating some fresh, delicious peaches and cherries and pears. We're having a late lunch of just fruit, looking up at the ancient being that is the snow-covered mountain directly in front of us.

"How many mysteries are in that mountain?" I ask her, cleaning off my juicy fingers. "I mean, just imagine if they wrote them all down one by one on a cedar-bark scroll, just how long do you think that scroll would be?"

Kids play on the giant tree-swing behind us, others feed the nearby goats, and another couple not too far away eats their fruit and has their own quiet romantic conversation. We'd come here last year with my girlfriend's parents, exploring, enjoying ourselves, and now we've come here just the two of us as a day-trip for our anniversary. Oregon is packed full of breathtaking sights and cool small towns nestled into all of the Nature.

"The lodge up there is where they filmed the opening to Stanley Kubrick's *The Shining*, isn't it?"

My girlfriend remembers something that is totally of interest to me, that I sort of forgot. I grab another plump cherry from our large bag.

"Yup. Stanley could probably sense some of the darker mysteries of the mountain. The wrath, the unexplained disappearances, the mountain's disappointment with the modern people who are just destroying the world he's been watching all these years."

We eat our fruit and drink our water and take in the majestic formation of rock, its heft and beauty, its strong, undeniable presence, its unfathomable oldness. Here are the ones we Natives remember to respect. Here are the ones we make our offerings to and sing our prayers to, following the wisdom of our ancestors.

"Do we have time to go there, you think?" she asks, closing up our mostly eaten bag of fruit.

"Realistically," I say, gazing at the drifts of snow, the shadows on the mountain, "probably we don't. Probably not today."

SHIELDING US, LIFTING US UP

My youth was full of violence, abuse,
and horror, and yet I'm constantly finding
moments where the ancestors were shielding
me and lifting me up.

Tree-covered, rooftop hideouts where my friends and I
listened to our cassette tapes; teachers who saw
how hurt I was but praised what they knew
would be my saving, my art; how the
Loup River washed me and held me in joy when
I went for a swim.

I remember going to church with my grandma
and asking her why grandpa didn't come
with us. "He believes," she said, "but
he believes in his own way."

My youth was a microcosm of our Native
People's story. All of the glaring things
meaning to destroy us will never be a
match for all of the invisible hands that're
there to protect us.

A message written in light on the darkness
of the night sky: You Didn't Come Here To
Die, Grandchild. You Came Here To Live.

FROM MY MIXED-UP FILES

Being the only Ponca family in New York City in the sixties was rough. Don't get me wrong: we were surrounded by a surging ocean of diversity, but being the only ones of your kind comes with an undeniable pain that just never leaves you.

But I want to talk less about that and more about one of the wildest adventures me and my kid brother Ray ever had in that big, magnificent city; I want to tell the tale of the time the two of us ran away and managed to secretly live in the Metropolitan Museum of Art for a full, action-packed week. Can you picture it? Two Ponca kids having the time of their lives after-hours in the moody, overflowing art-realm of one of the world's greatest museums. Two Ponca kids standing in front of that famous mural depicting all 8,000 individual faces of the Indians who were marched on the Trail of Tears, eating our candy bars in a fort made of backroom Warhols, outsmarting the nightwatchman who kind of looked like an Indian himself.

Don't you think such tales need to be told, to be written down for the entertainment and edification of others, Indians and the general public? I do.

So, that being said, grab your tea and get cuddled up under your favorite blanket, because it's time to follow my brother and me into some New York City immortality. It's time to put our runaway adventure moccasins on and go!

DIGGING IN

I'm constantly imagining different
circumstances, peering into how it
could've all played out differently.

Like what if there had been several
Ponca medicine men to help me
when I was young, to help me to
understand my gift?

Or what if our reservation hadn't
been broken up and sold out from
under us and we still had some
massive piece of our original lands
that had never left us through
all of this?

Somehow I believe that dipping into
this pool of possibilities empowers
me to unleash the best maneuvers
and gameplans for my people now,
from this very moment forward.

I believe it's okay to feel my wounds
and dream as powerfully as if I've
always had everything my Ponca soul
has ever needed too.

That's why I constantly find myself
imagining different circumstances.

THE ALCHEMIST'S RIBS

The last century had been so vicious that we crawled into the corpse of a bear we'd found frozen on the Plains. Inside we found saws, mugs, magazines, an expired alchemist with a door in his ribs, and being crawlers, we crawled into him. In that man we found stolen Ponca tears that our grandparents were meant to cry when they were kids and being of the mind to set things right whenever we could, we cried those tears for them, sobbing until the earth shook. After we explored all of that strange alchemist's possessions, we tunneled into an underground castle he was attached to and saw all sorts of ghosts that were operating the back rooms of his psyche. We dispatched as many of them as we could, each of us sacrificing even a finger to obliterate a few more, and then, somehow, we were riding rafts of dense moss down dark waters into the center of a mountain that hadn't felt the stars in ages. Bats nuzzled us, otters with blue eyes guided us, crocodiles spat out strange foods for us that were as tasty as anything we'd ever eaten. We traveled for weeks like this, having a good time, feeling happy, seeing creatures that hadn't been seen by human eyes in centuries, knocking off the knobby tips of stalactites for fun. Then we grew impossibly lonesome for our old, Poncas-under-siege-in-the-21st-century-life. We fell into the brutally cold waters and swam down until we found a substance to dig and then crawl in and through. We crawled until our fingertips pressed out into the open prairie air and then we stopped, savored our strange journey, then poured out again onto the frozen ground. Everything was sparkling, smoldering, like glitter and lava. We heard howls in the distance, drumming and tiny human voices. Having fewer fingers than what we started with, we hugged ourselves and set off towards the silence in the other direction.

A REMEMBERED DREAM OF JOY'S TOTALITY

My favorite Native book I've read is Rex Iron Thunder's *A Remembered Dream of Joy's Totality*. It's several volumes, just an astonishing achievement. If you're not familiar with it, it is a complete record of every moment of joy that has ever been experienced by every Ponca who has ever lived. I am in awe that such a book even exists. It will be medicine for all Indigenous People and for all of humanity for as long as books and our species are around.

I personally love reading the long chapters that document my bloodline's joy, from long before the White Man came to the 80s when I was growing up. Moments that could not be rendered by anyone but a writer of Rex Iron Thunder's caliber. Encounters with dinosaurs, reflections by the Niobrara on a lost summer night, my dad running in Norfolk when he hadn't fully hardened yet. I can very easily say that I'll never love another book like I love this one.

If you do anything after reading through all that I've written in the preceding four thousand pages, I pray that you acquire yourself a copy of this miraculous book. Imbibe my tribe's joy and I promise you will be changed.

THE DEER AND I MEET EYES

When I head out to work in the mornings
I often see a local deer friend sitting
like a peaceful living statue by our sweatlodge.

I get in our car and look at him and
he looks at me, both of us trying to divine
the other's thoughts.

It's a great tragedy afflicting the entire
world, how much people have lost their
friendships with the plants and animals
of the world, how much that connection has
been tossed into the landfill with everything else.

I fire up our Subaru and enjoy those moments
in our backyard, where the tragedy surrounds
us but is not the main storyteller,
where the deer and I are daily reversing
the curse.

We meet eyes, and then he returns to
his grass and I take off to work, to
make some money so that I can have
something nice to eat too.

PART TWO

A KERNEL OF PONCA CORN

I have one kernel of Ponca corn
tattooed on my inner forearm.
It's the only tattoo I have.

It's an eye, a doorway, a signal,
an inheritance, a reminder of what
we Ponca carry, a bible with

no words that tells me exactly
why I'm here.

PITTOCK

I took a picture of my book
where it was on display in the
belly of this Portland mansion
as part of this Native Art show

and these two non-Native guys
were reading about the boarding schools
behind me, saying, "That
ain't right what was done

to those Indian kids. That
was horrible, pure evil." I
stayed silent. Running around
in the room to our left

were a bunch of wild young
Native kids, while standing all
around us were other young
Native kids: ones without

voices, from that other time,
who never went home, or who
were never the same when they finally
did. "It was fucked up," I said

to myself, getting out of there, going
to look at some of the art in
another part of the show. "It was
all really fucked up."

UNIMAGINABLE INDIGENOUS BEAUTY

I know I'm not the only Native
who thinks that if I just write enough
I might be able to transform

all of these colonizing, soul-killing
beasts into air and old postcards
and corpses for compost and

apology-filled allies and the
stuff of the past. I know I'm
not the only Native writing to

call in a miracle, make things right,
put my ancestors' knowledge in the
code, defy all the designs and

turn the future into a flood of
unimaginable Indigenous beauty.
I know I'm not the only Native

who's writing my ass off in service
to that impossible, inevitable
dream. I know I'm not the

only one.

WHEN INDIAN FATHERS SWIM
WITH THEIR INDIAN SONS

I can't remember the last time
my dad and I ever went swimming
together. I can't remember if

we *ever* went swimming together.
We Indian sons are always thinking
of our Indian dads. To be Indian

is to be born into a strange, violent,
beautiful mystery; and for us boys
our dads are one of the big keys

to understanding that mystery. My
dad was a fighter, a convict, an
alcoholic, a drug-dealer. I'm glad

he's still alive. We didn't talk for
10 years and now we stay in touch.
We're both named Cliff. We really

love each other. Maybe there's even
time left for us to go swimming
together.

OPENING PROCEDURES
AT THE CO-OP

I arrive at the Co-op at 7am
to get the store ready to open at 8.
I take down the chairs in the deli
seating area inside and then go outside
and set up the chairs there, saying hi
to the plants, hoping the sun comes out
today.
On my way back in I cross paths with
our cleaning lady, who comes in at 6,
earliest of all.
As I lock the door, she says, "Make
sure you lock that good. We don't
want any of the Natives sneaking in
here early."
My Native ears perk up.
She toddles off with her broom.
We've got to rewrite the code of the
culture; we've got to rewrite the
script.
I feel a slash from one of the demigods
who've been out to kill us all since Columbus
came here; wipe the blood from my neck.
I set up the can return area, unlock
the carts, turn on the TVs, fill the

spray bottles, and then go outside to
yell and then pray and then
sing.

THE LUCKY MUD

I get up to piss in the middle
of the night and step outside of
the tiny house (shack really) we're
staying in, closing the door on my

sleeping partner behind me. Moonlight
colors everything, the heavy trees,
the wild commune yard, our friend's
sinking trailer, the ground beneath

my bare feet. I direct my stream
away from the tiny house, feel the
cold air on my road-weary body,
fall some into the magic of how

we got here, listen to the lovely
country night-time quiet. I'm
a penniless artist, a voyager,
a learning lover, a man with no

more piss left. I stay there
for one more moment enjoying
the encompassing painting of the place
and then I return to the warmth

of our too-small bed and gratefully
go back to sleep.

THUNDER HEAD

The first photograph of a Ponca still exists. It's treated with much more care than the bones of my people or my people themselves, for that matter. It's in a glass case in the Great Plains Museum in Omaha, Nebraska. I've only seen it in person once.

It's a picture of Thunder Head, an old man that I've never found anything else about. He's bulky, veined, adorned in Ponca clothes as we knew them before we knew any non-Natives. He looks proud, sad, distracted. (The edges of the photograph are dirty, aged; that always catches my eye.) A man capable of things we've now forgotten, familiar with things we can't imagine. The kind of man who could make a flute out of an animal bone and play a song to the small creatures hiding in the grass by the river on the last day of the harshest, whitest moon.

I imagine Thunder Head's picture traveling to distant galaxies in a tiny capsule a thousand years from now. Intact in its case. Rustling, raging, a vector of immortal Plains poetry. Ready to speak when he encounters the right kind of being who's ready to listen.

TAKING OVER THE NEW YORKER

I open up a copy of The New Yorker and discover that the issue is written entirely by Native writers. Is this a dream?

I drink my coffee and flip through it, begin reading pieces here and there. This is what I live for: when big institutions like this radically throw their weight behind the Indigenous cause, when they offer themselves up to be completely remade by us Natives.

My partner comes into the kitchen, groggy and in her pajamas. "Reading already?"

I feel like a reverse Native apocalypse is happening on Turtle Island, like everyone holding this week's New Yorker in their hands is a piece of landscape changing back into the pure prairie, buffalo, original tribal language.

I sip my coffee again. "Reading like a beast, feeling like an angel," I say.

She squints at me, grabbing a cup.

"And looking like a Native," she says, "who's ready to fucking rock."

SWIMMING FOR THE MOST POWERFUL MEMORY

What is the one collective Ponca memory that could step to the forefront to become the irresistible thing that alters the course of our maniacal civilization?

Is there such a memory and could it possibly be endowed with such power?

I sit in my car by the river (my 'office' during covid) and swim back through the layers of time, calling out in all directions for that singular memory to come to me, so that I can witness it, hold it in my arms, put it in my medicine pack, bring it like an ancient living artwork into the organism of our present.

I stare out the window, watch the passing container ships, the families on the riverwalk, and search my tribe's collective for that memory. Something is telling me it's there. Something is telling me to keep going, to find it, to bring it back. Something is telling me that such a thing has been the deepest purpose of memory itself all along.

THE RED ROADERS

My girlfriend and I see a stately spotted eagle perched on the very top of a nearby tree while we're out for a walk. It's still, sharp, almost hallucinatory; looking out over the moving waters of the Columbia River.

We stand and gawk in awe. Eagles are better than just about all of the junk everyone in our society is frantically chasing after. Eagles communicate the presence of the shining reality behind all things. Appreciate them and you train yourself to appreciate all of the sacred mysteries whirling among us. At least that's how we Red Roaders see them.

"Have you ever touched a tree with an eagle in it?" I ask her, watching the eagle remain in their stillness even as we continue to stand there and admire them. I asked the question because I myself never had.

"No," my girlfriend says, visibly beginning to sparkle with a white and blue light the longer she peers up at the eagle.

"Then maybe you should now."

She looks at me. "Really?"

I shrug my shoulders, wondering if this will be the day when my super-fantasy of having a wild eagle drop a single feather into my very hands comes true.

My girlfriend walks over the railroad tracks, through the snotty-nosed bramble, and quietly makes her way up to the tree. She leans in, places her hands on the speckled white bark, lowers her head in prayer.

The eagle remains.

I crane my neck up at the eagle and then drop my gaze down to my girlfriend, taking in the moment, allowing it to stain my insides. "It only took 41 years," I hear myself saying. "41 years to touch a tree with a wild and free eagle in it."

SURPRISE'S BROWN SAP

I woke up covered in the brown
sap of surprise, a sticky, captured

mess. It got me every couple
of days, it got us all. But

if we weren't here for the surprises
what would we be here for?

Could mean seeing an old enemy,
could mean a check in the mail,

could mean walking in on a beautifully
fluttering flock of butterflies in

the Co-op bathroom. I yanked
my bed stuff off, jumped into

the shower. The sap ran from
my skin, gummed up the drain,

emitted almost a faint jazzy
music as it finally, eventually left.

I turned and swiveled under
the hot water, clean and a

tiny bit energized. Maybe I
secretly loved the sap, getting

gooed. I mean, a surprise meant
something was going to happen in

this grinding world and don't
we all just long for something

different to happen?

CLAW MARKS IN STONE

In the distance roam the infinitely hungry monsters who won't cross the bubbling, purple river that divides these parts; scratching, sucking, screaming, searching for morsels like him.

Caped in black-tipped, indestructible eagle feathers, everything above his waist painted clay-red except the oval of his face, dressed in skins, and armed with a lightweight, deadly bow, he walks and scans and senses for pieces of the old story, for things from before the monsters came.

Hours pass. He studies the grass, the charred, beautiful shrubs with their intricate flowers, listens to the man in the pebble in the pouch around his neck who sometimes provides commentary on the gashed earth he's found himself in.

Up close the varieties of far-enough-away monsters would dwarf him, like a tentacled bear to a brown mouse, but from his side of the river they're spinning shapes, shrieking puppets, netherworldly bits leaping and disappearing behind the twisted trees.

His pebble tells him to 'go still and look at the river.'

He stops, unfolds his spy-glass and peers into the plagued river, seeing nothing but heaving, stinking waves of things trying to get out.

And then: a smooth form rises from the purple, like carved white marble, a shining torso without head or limbs, drawn upwards by an ancient ache that he could immediately feel.

It hangs there, slowly rotating in the misty space.

'Retrieve it,' the pebble man says.

'Its song is worth knowing.'

SEEDS WITHIN SEEDS

In the future Natives won't
have to spend as much time
trying to make peace with and

accepting all the ways they were
abused, silenced, and overlooked
when they were young. Instead

they'll be flush with radical
opportunities from the get-go
and they'll look back feeling

good about how they were born
in a time when things were
finally, mostly decent and

right and just for Natives.
They'll reflect on the times
that we're working towards now

and be as proud of us as we
are of our own ancestors.

ANCIENT EQUALS VIVID

I sit on our couch and wonder
if I'll ever completely lose
these vivid memories
that come to visit me.

I suppose I will but
until then I'll keep my loyalty
to them; keep my faith.

Our humanity desires to pour
forward into our consciousness
to make sure that we remember
how beautiful we all are.

We've got to allow it,
like the owl at our window
that really does have something
important to say.

The modern world wishes
we'd just reach for some junk food
or our phone but every other
ancient creature on earth

is praying that when the vividness
comes we'll stop and reach for it
with both of our arms.

LEO YANKTON

Does every Native feel the compulsion
to remember every Native they've
known who's ever died?
A part of me just wants to write
about all these relatives I've known
who are no longer around.
Our memory is our lifeline
to the unkillable thing that
bonds us all together.
I bet a long time ago
some part of us all saw what was coming
and a decision was made to put
all of our energy into the force
of our remembering, like we
set it up so that our remembering
of each other would continue on
above all else.
I remember talking to Leo Yankton
at the coffee shop, him telling
me about a Native fantasy novel
he had written about a young boy
and his unicorn—
"Just needs another draft
and an editor," he said.
"I'd love to read it," I said,
my imagination opening up.

Leo was tall, handsome, a protector,
a father, raised by his grandma.
He looked past me, saw someone,
saw something; maybe that brown-
skinned boy on his unicorn waving
to him.
"I'd love to have you read it," he said.
"I really believe this book could help
a lot of children someday."

A ROSE IN TEXAS HILL COUNTRY

I stood on the edge of the shaggy bluff in Texas as the wedding guests gathered and assembled behind me, looking out at the view of the desert, ranch buildings, and cloud-filled skies. Its sweet immensity was taking me somewhere; where, I didn't know, but I could feel it.

Then, as I was spiriting out, a stranger stepped up beside me and said, "You don't see that in Nebraska, do you?"

It was a wedding party of 200 people and I only knew the smallest handful of them, pretty much just my girlfriend's immediate family. Reality bent around me. To be identified as a Nebraskan by a complete stranger in the hill country of Texas?

I turned to the guy. He was older, with a face that had folds in it. He was smiling.

"I'm from Nebraska. Did you know that?"

His eyes went big. "No, I didn't. It's just a saying. 'You don't see that in Nebraska.'"

Something inside of me felt the spirits winking at me, reassuring me that the prayers I'd been making on this trip had been heard.

"Well, I'm from Nebraska and you're right: you sure don't see nothing like this back there. Lots of flat cornfields but nothing close to this."

We both looked out onto the beauty of the land, sharing a moment, my girlfriend laughing with a cousin a few feet away, a hairy musician tuning his guitar in a tree's shadow to our right.

"What a place," I said, breathing deeply.

I turned to say something else to the guy but he was gone, melted back into all of the other well-dressed guests behind us. I rejoined my girlfriend, smiling, sweating, feeling just a touch more ready for what was to come.

MAGIC, GRIEF, ART

Graphic Novel Panel: I'm in the backseat of a van some friends have rented, seeing this magnificent fully Native Don Quixote sculpture proudly erupting from some roadside taco joint. I'm young, skinny, with a mullet and glasses. There's an earthy, professorial little person puffing on a pipe squeezed in beside me, and then a ghost buffalo's reflection in the window too. The Native Don Quixote is blazing, a wildly put together, hand-built emissary from a world we all can just feel around the edges of this mainstream American one we're all stuck in. Magic, grief, art, the road, big figures, spirit-helpers, the destinies our young people carry. A thought balloon hangs by my head, reading: "Indians are everywhere and still no one can see them."

BEAR MAN ON THE EVENING TELEVISION

I remember watching this Inuit guy
get interviewed on TV one night
when I was maybe 10 years old
about how he survived a night

in the freezing waters of the arctic.
He said he called on the spirit of the
bear and felt that bear's big furry body
keeping him warm and alive through

what should've been a deadly and impossible
night. He was on the show we were watching
because his survival couldn't be explained,
and his story was that of a 'primitive,' a

First Nations person saying he was saved
by a Bear Spirit. I believed. I sat on our
trailer's living room floor and didn't
understand how such things worked

but I believed they did. He should've
been dead and lost but he was still
with his family practicing his traditional ways.
I watched him talk and felt with

the soul of my young self how the
spirits were real and how they could
intervene and save us.

SLOPPY BUTTERFLIES IN THE
FOREST MOONLIGHT

Certain books are rites of passage. And without a doubt the best such book for us Natives is Maynard Jackson's (Warm Springs) *Sloppy Butterflies in the Forest Moonlight.*

What a hot, unreal, eye-opening, piece of unforgettable Native erotica that short story collection was for me when I read it as a teenager in Columbus. Natives of all shapes and sizes having sex in all different time-periods, polluted cites, assimilation, 60s counter-culture, delicate fantasy worlds that didn't exist. Reading about my people and their charged sex lives sprouted a kind of hope in me that's been a part of my being ever since, and even after I myself became an adult with a graphically real, graphically indescribable sex life of my own. The nature of Jackson's descriptions are of the sweetest literary gifts the gods have been able to smuggle into this world for the Native masses in this modern age. I remember reading it in the quiet of the public library and my mind became like a luminous dome of gorgeous wet protuberances, all longing for the myriad kinds of sexual connections, delights, and ecstasies folded into that book's bittersweet pages.

I still have my copy, flip through it like a soul-memoir that Turtle Island herself wrote, and feel the sex in it like sweat and multiple orgasms and lightning.

LET IT RIP

What would our Native people
look like today if we hadn't
suffered so much abuse?
What would our force in the
world look like?
What purpose would our
unfolding stories serve?

I gallop on the back of a
buffalo across the Plains
thinking about these things,
cop cars and military vehicles
in hot pursuit.

They say I'm dangerous
to the life of the monsters
they're all locked into feeding
because I'm writing this
book.

I shoot my medicine arrows into
the wide-open sky, puncturing
anything that's trying to seal-off
our hope-

And I yell back, "I bet you
say that to all the braves
you see riding on the backs
of badass buffalo like this!"

MODERN MUTANT ODDITIES

If there were some National holiday
where every Native bought themselves
a present (a decent amount of money
allocated to all so they could get
something good), I wonder what
would be the most popularly
purchased thing?
Clothes, a car, jewelry, books,
a TV, a house, a canoe,
a few days back home, a piece
of their people's original homelands?
How would our grief dance through
this shadowy world on that holiday?
What would the economically better-off
think of our choices, how would they
judge us, how would they empathize?
What would the ancestors whisper to us
to do on that day with our handful
of loot?
What would we say about ourselves
with our living out of this yet another
modern mutant oddity of an experience?
Everyone, including us, sees what was
the most purchased thing this year,
puts a hand to their thumping chest,
shivers for a second, and says,
"Again?"

THE LAKOTA WHO WAS THERE

I was 18 and knew not a single person on campus. I walked around, explored the library, just kept going on as a sad, quiet outsider because I've always had the will to keep going.

Repeating myself, I went back to the Union, descended the stairs to a small common area where a big TV was playing to no one (how unimaginably different my college life would've been had I made any friends). I sat down in the semi-darkness and just let time pass, floating with nothing better to do.

Then, this skinny old Lakota guy wandered in, scared, a face so scarred up it was hard to look at, obviously homeless. He introduced himself, sat down beside me with his bag, and began talking to me. This was my first street Native I'd meet in my eventual 15 years of knowing all the street Natives in Lincoln (to all of you now on the Other Side, you are remembered, you are loved, and this pour of coffee's for you).

"...I was there at Wounded Knee, holding a rifle and watching the Government line their tanks up against us. I know a lot of people look at me and think I'm nothing but I was there, you know, ready to die for our people..."

Even at that age I could feel when the Big History of our people was speaking through someone; when it was handing me something to put into my satchel for safekeeping.

"Do you have a dollar so that I could get something to drink, kola?" he asked, part almost ghoulish, part pure unsung hero among all of us dreamy-headed college kids.

I reached into my pocket where I had literally just a few dollars and gave him one.

"Thank you. I don't know how I'd survive without the couple bucks people give me here and there."

I smiled like it was all I had because it kind of was.

He grabbed his bag and left, leaving me to ponder what he'd shared, to feel the drops of bloody history that were trailing him.

ANIMATED PETROGLYPHS

I spirit-travel to the far-off future where our globe-spanning civilization has been properly recentered around humanity's foundational Indigenous knowing. People are hauntingly the same there, and utterly different somehow too. My time-point origination gives off a shade of light blue that is rare and curious to them.

I pass through a gelatinous membrane circled by an underground gateway braided of stones and plants and then moving pieces of technology that seem alive in ways nothing of our time does. A group of dark-skinned men greet me, one of them pounding on a two-faced kid's drum to create a medium with his song that allows us all to communicate easier.

I turn into a cloud of animated petroglyphs, a talking Ponca elder's face, a boy with songs flowering out of my body, a bonnetted warrior hovering in the colorful emanations of their medicine doings. I receive most of what they collectively desire to give me about the equational cord of happenings that resulted in their civilization-form before too much of our actual talking begins.

Like an enchanted wind, I blow into their minds, get to know them all at once. "These abilities were why the colonizers of your time couldn't afford to let you live," a wolfen soldier-type says. "They wanted your land, yes, but they wanted to extinguish the keepers of their...Kryptonite even more so."

I spin and weave like sand, concentrate into a plurality of telepathic beams, grow into steel and stars and the memories of my ancestors.

I chuckle, as real as what is really being given to me, and say, "Go on..."

SEASONS (WAITING ON YOU)

Amanda and I walked up 17th street towards downtown with purpose, talking a thousand miles an hour, burning up in the summer sun. I was a handful of years older and in some ways we were a mismatched pair, but in other ways we were a perfect package. I was a spiritual Native hard-up for some fresh friends, a writer and a poet, and she was a hardcore, hairy-legged feminist poet community activist with just the sweetest, most sensual, hope-filled fish swimming in the story-lake of her heart. We were so lucky to find each other; I was so lucky to have found her (I'd been growing more and more colorless and heartsick with an unshakable loneliness for years). It's the stuff of true miracles how we find our kindred-spirit friends and lovers with whom we wind up spending some of our best and most critical times with. I mean, without such people, who would we be and what would this life be?

"Do you feel like we should maybe have one beer at O'Rourke's tonight?" I asked her, not sure which one of us was actually responsible for the fast pace we were keeping, but trucking along like I was about to start running nevertheless.

"Beer plus jukebox plus dancing before the place gets too full does equal my kind of ecstasy," she said back, pushing her thick black-rimmed glasses back up her nose. I admired her for a second, always able to see how pretty she really was even if she was in a bit of a personal war against such things.

"We better hurry up," she said, skip dancing ahead, bored, loud traffic ripping by.

"Are you kidding?" I asked, flexing something Indian inside myself because I was always sort of enthusiastically doing that. "I'm about to collapse in this desert sun!"

"Just think of how cold that beer'll be. The froth. The icy glass in our hand. There are things worth picking up the pace for. Let's burn some shoe leather!"

Down the sidewalk we went, not dating, hungry for so much, getting by with each other on another passing Lincoln summer's day.

BURIAL WAYS

What things were your ancestors
buried with that you want to

be buried with today? What
things can you do today to

make sure that your children and descendants
stand a good chance of being buried

with some of what your ancestors
were buried with? I remember

sitting on an uncomfortable chair
in the Indian Center and listening to

a medicine man tell me about
something he was planning on being

buried with. The gap between
the past and the present really is

as small as it is big. Maybe
you will be proudly buried

with things you don't even
know of today. Maybe you

will be richly decked out
and buried with holy things

just like your ancestors.

BOOK PEOPLE

I searched the shelves in the Austin bookstore for something to plunge into, to excitedly fly home with. But time was running out. The store was closing in 15 minutes.

I talked with the crowd of Natives who were all loudly jaw-jacking but nothing fell into my hands. I had a little martial arts fight with a bushy-headed wilderness lover but he didn't pass the test. I found spots where much-desired novels were missing from the shelves and hung my head, whispered my disappointment into the dark night-time earth. I smashed popcorn and quaffed paranormal brews with my graphic novel inhabitants and still found nothing promising levitating my way.

I wandered, I imagined, I lusted, I dreamed, I listened like a fox for faraway hints of welcomed, coming visitors, I became books, then a patchwork Ponca Frankenstein, then a romantic feeling traversing the space of a tattooed barista's heart that the younger me would've for sure had a crush on. And still nothing.

Aislinn and I walked out of the store, the last customers of the night, and began walking to the nearby Whole Foods.

"You didn't find anything you liked?" she asked, both a new book and a new journal in her hand.

I shook my head and sighed.

"Nope, I guess not."

We walked in the buzzing silence, all of the new friends I almost took home with me waving goodbye from their dark, closed windows.

REMEMBERING FORWARD

I can remember things from
my future and you can too.
The smallest details of what
happened to me as a kid in
Nebraska read their comics
in the other room but just
as clearly the healed future
sits with me and my pipe
right here in this room.
Peer forward through the lens
of your innermost heart's hope
and remember what's coming
to dismantle this failing empire
of pain.
Listen to what the spirits
ahead of you are saying and
remake this life you're carrying
right now.

GRANDMA HELEN

I go to visit the little place in Verdel my dad's always telling me about, the place where he visited his grandma as a kid, before she was tragically taken from him in a car wreck.

It's so small it'd be called a tiny home nowadays, something like a four-sided nub with windows and a line of smoke coming out of its roof. The sunlight feels like 1962. Nobody here knows me. Because of the time I'm coming from I'm practically invisible to them.

I walk up to a set of windows on the side and see my great-grandma, toiling away, several shades darker than me, surrounded by a host of even older Indians that I can see but she can only feel. She looks busy, grumpy, happy; she doesn't know that her life is going to be cut short, not yet. I allow some of my heart-feelings to move through the wall, to mix with the others who're keeping her company and entertained. "This is from my dad," I whisper.

Growing up, my dad shared just about nothing from his past, his mustached lips were painfully sealed shut. As I became an adult, entering my thirties and then forties, he began to let just a few couple-sentence-long stories slip through. He always talked about his Ponca grandma that life stole from him at a young age. "She was going to raise me like a true Ponca," he said, drinking his beer. "She was going to raise me in the traditional way."

I stand and watch this grandma whom I never knew as she cooks and remembers a time that all of us Poncas would give an arm to know in its fullness. She stirs potatoes on the cook stove, laughs at a joke that's part hers and part the invisible people's who're standing around her. Some blue-white energy is radiating off of her pure black hair and I reach for it, reach to know it so that I can at least know something about her.

"It's Cliff," I say, feeling her hair's energy. "It's me…"

GRANDMA CLEO

Every time another Native grandma
leaves this world the whole being

of our Mother Earth feels it.
Grandma Cleo has left and I

feel it out here in Astoria.
Sitting with her in her shade tent

at her brother's Sundance while she
worked on her beadwork, me

knowing nobody, her talking to me
like she'd raised me since I was

little, loving like that. So
many places to go in my memories—

how painful it is not being able to
make the funeral, what she means

to the story of my life, descriptions
of my times with her—but

what would she want? I go
in through the back door of her and

grandpa Dean's house in Omaha,
saying hello and giving them both

a hug, so happy to have grandparents
like them in my life, so grateful

to be a part of their family. "How
are you doing, grandma Cleo?"

I ask. "It's good to see you. Got
any coffee?" The earth quakes

and for awhile, doing like we do,
we remember her and miss her and

weep.

DEER, CORN, AND LIGHTNING

Graphic Novel Page: a chubby but tough Ponca in moccasins, shorts, and wearing a patch-covered backpack, is pulling what looks like an impossibly large blanket behind him in the desert, on which appear to be thousands of other Poncas of every age, size, gender, and sort imaginable. It's blisteringly hot out. All the Poncas on the blanket are either sleeping, in a state of suspended animation, or dead—somehow it's not clear. The chubby Ponca is not the man for the task he's locked into but he's also clearly becoming that man as he takes it on. Outlines of a futuristic civilization in ruins are scrawled on the horizon in the distance. Maybe the eye of one little baby is open among the mass of Poncas being pulled, shining, like a secret that tells more about everything than the tough Ponca knows. There are dunes ahead. He can't possibly last much longer. He grits his teeth and drags his tribe behind him, unable to get good footing, with a word balloon by his sweaty head that says, "This is NOT the end. It just can't be."

THE SPEAR OF LONGING

I'm 33 and after several hours
on a Friday night at the coffee shop
I say see ya later to my other buddies
and walk down the strip mall to the
last Blockbuster in town.
I walk the aisles, consider the box
covers, read some backs, feel how
much I long for a partner to be
looking for a movie with, watch
my longing spear through the ceiling
actually, revealing the dark Nebraskan
night.
I settle on an indie film, rent it
from the lively dreadlocked cashier,
find my dented car in the parking lot,
and drive back to my quiet apartment.
I park, walk past the nearby bar,
go inside and think about how I've
comforted myself through my Friday night
loneliness like this for years, watching
movies, dreaming myself into them,
nobody to be with as the hours pass
but myself and the things I won't
give up on.
I sit on my recliner, press play,
and drift around as the previews for

other movies go by one after another.
I shudder and rally and swim
through the bodies of my curse,
sad, grateful, pained, hopeful.
My movie finally begins and
as if I'm talking to a spirit-friend
who's watching the movie with me
from their place on my old couch,
I ask aloud, "So is this
the life of an Indigenous Futurist?"
The television fills and in a matter
of minutes I've forgotten entirely
about both my question and the fact
that no one's answered me at all.

NEBRASKA: 1952

We sat in her pickup truck on the side of a country road up in Knox County. The mosquitos were out. The heat was heavy.

"What is it made of?" I asked, holding the little bluish bone-like lens to my eye.

"We don't know. We only know that it's old."

I looked at it in my hand for a bit, felt a shiver rattlesnake through me. Back home where there should've been two older brothers there were only the unspoken things about the two sons who were both trying not to die in Korea. I didn't understand the object in my hand; I didn't understand anything.

She swallowed, didn't look at me. "You put it on your eyeball, try to pull a piece of your eyelid over it."

"Really? Isn't that kind of crazy?"

"It's old Indian stuff. You can't be afraid."

I looked out at the grasses and the river, at a butterfly poking around by the nose of the pickup. "We're here to die," I heard my dad say in my mind, his Santee accent thick and portentous.

I slowly put the misshapen coin-sized lens thing to my eye, closed both eyes, touched my eyeball and tried not to scream, gently forced some lid over the thing, was sucked back and pulled forward simultaneously.

"What do you see?" she said from faraway.

Murmurs of Indians talking on the edges of something tunneling through space, bars of soft light, belches of images

I knew but that were too painful to fully let myself recognize. Waves of people leaving a village with lines of music arcing out of their heads into the heads of other Indians in remixed tribal attire who're manipulating floating blocks of delicate, fluid controls on a craft that's passing through galaxies, seeds of things not currently understood to have physical forms stacked up in their cargo. Birds melting. An Indian woman talking to the land; the land vibrating, making her shudder, step back, talk some more. The Indians in the craft laughing, materializing small items from their hands for a game, like crystal dice maybe, humming in the middle of so much vast, music-filled space. Eyes looking back—

I plunked the thing out and down onto the floorboards of the truck, down by my feet.

"Ah! What—"

She leaned over and took back the object.

"Grandpa said the future wants to talk to us just as much as the past does. Grandpa says all sorts of things like these are coming back."

I looked over at her and didn't know what to say. The wind moved the world behind her. Inside, I was afraid, I was silent, and I knew that her grandpa was right.

YOUNGS RIVER FALLS

We visit Youngs River Falls and
as my girlfriend scales some boulders
in the mist like a curious oracle
on the scent of something, I wonder
about how the Natives here a long time ago
saw, understood, related to, and
comprehended this waterfall—
I wonder what their name for it is
and how that name came to be.

Through a prayerful silence I do my
best to visit with this robust
waterfall that hasn't gone anywhere
even if our true knowledge of its sentient
totality seemingly has, vanished among
the minds of nearly all of its contemporary
visitors.

I sink, slither, pause, open wings,
contemplate, delight, pour words,
aspire, appreciate, nuzzle, smile,
inquire, let go, return to my
chubby body and stay in the
beautiful communal silence.

My girlfriend joins me on my perch,
(something new from her climb

in her breast too), we hold hands,
and lean on each other in the shadows
and the light of the waterfall's endless
spray.

THE THREE CLIFFS

My dad and I stop at my
grandpa Taylor's grave in
Norfolk.
We stand there in the sun
and wind and think and
remember.
My dad was in prison when
my grandpa passed, unable
to help bury him and
place him into the
ground.
Neither one of us cries even
though at least one of us
could if the other went
first.
How do us two Cliffs
look to that oldest Cliff
up there in the sky?
What's he thinking about
the two of us?
What can he see that
we can't?
I kneel down and put a
little plastic Bigfoot on
his marker, some tobacco and
some sage.

My dad carries family stories
that I'd deeply, deeply
love to know, but he says
nothing.
Our visit is short.
We get back on the road,
closer than ever, the past
never talked about.
"You got everything you need
for Sundance?" my dad
asks.
"I think so," I say.
"If we need to we can
always run to the Walmart
in Yankton," he says.
"They got just about
everything you could need."

CONNECTIONS STRONGER THAN PAIN

Lift up your mind and place it
in the mindscape of your strongest
ancestors.
Allow yourself to see through their eyes
just as they're constantly seeing through
your eyes.
Let the rain of their love drizzle down
into your heart and make it fresh
and hopeful and brave again.
Keep your mind up there long enough
to make sure your connection to them
is stronger than your connection to money,
pain, or the bullshit of these times.
Feel that glow of the togetherness you
share with them and resolve to have
that glow in your entire body and life.
And then when the time's right
carefully, tenderly bring your mind
back down from the grace of their realm,
placing it back inside yourself
like a gift that they've blessed
with each and every single one
of their hands.

THE RIGHT HEADS ROLL

If we didn't have 80s horror movies like The Right Heads Roll, this world would just be unbearable and too damn hard to live in.

Sometimes there is a genius bigger than us operating through us and that must've totally been the case with screenwriter Winston Black and his painfully accurate and wildly satisfying entry into the genre classics of that era. It is just so revolutionary to see a horror film set on the Ponca reservation at the turn of the century, to provide viewers with scenes that're so true as to shatter the shell of historical misinformation that has been poured like toxic concrete around the soul of people here in America; and then the gory creature-feature that follows and splatters up those scenes is just so smartly executed and uncompromisingly Native as to deliver delicious truth after delicious truth to those souls who're just beginning to see some real Native reality in an off-Hollywood movie for maybe the first time.

I love watching the smoking, black, cosmic creature eat the asshole ranchers in the beginning, and when the Poncas pull out all of their old weapons and gear for the supernatural, to save the white people who were never all that good at saving them, talking slow, meeting up in that shack, painting their faces, that's a sequence that got me through high school, desperate times in my twenties, and just long nights in general, over and over again. It's burned into me the way I want such things burned into me.

Reggie Hall, braided, built, with veins all up and down his dark brown hands and arms, pulls out his old bone blade that he says can't be broken, takes a sip of his coffee, and says, "Like this blade, we won't break," and you know what he's saying is the truth. Makes me shiver every time.

Horror movies have power but Native horror movies like this have something beyond power: they have what it takes to remake a broken world into a world worth living in.

NOVELIZATION OF THE RIGHT HEADS ROLL

From the novelization of The Right Heads Roll—

Pieces of the creature were levitating off of its wet, spiny back, into the unearthly night, but it wasn't becoming anything less; somehow it was becoming more—more able, more dense, more thirsty for white and Native blood.

Tommy ran toward it, crossing the bumpy field in his thin moccasins, a runner on a suicide mission who was fearless because he'd dreamed a long time ago that he was to have a beautiful life until a night of otherworldly carnage like this. In his hand were two medicine stones, white, like little moons, mind-disruptors for creatures not of this world that Old Man Roy had given him when his mom had been consumed by the creature the day before. They glowed and perspired in his hands as he got closer to the thing, as his spirit began to needle its pulsing aura. He was silent, determined; a warrior who'd been waiting for his time.

The creature unleashed an unholy scream and the whole land pulled back, grimacing over what was about to happen next.

ENORMOUS INDIGENOUS HEADS RISING FROM THE EARTH

I sat on my park bench surrounded by tourists, couples having picnics, street people, and Seattle folks just trying to get somewhere else fast. It was my day off and I had nowhere else to be, plus I was new enough to the city and knew so few other places, that this little waterside park with the enormous glowing Indian head planted in it seemed like just the place to be.

You had to give Seattle credit for being bold or even visionary enough to carve out such a sweet little park around such an imposing, communicative, undeniable expression of these land's original peoples. It's about two stories tall, as wide as a three-car garage, old-looking as the earth herself; the old man features are smooth, pitted, gray-brown, ageless; his face is knowingly thinking about something, reminding every viewer or passerby to get back in touch with what they really know too. A mohawked kid paused on his bike in front of the head and looked like a little bug next to a god's immortal, unbothered visage; was comical and slightly surreal too.

I sat my phone down beside me and wondered what the people in my hometown would've done had we had a similar giant old stone Indian statue in our park. Maybe spraypaint Bart Simpson on it, sledgehammer its nose off, tell their kids to stay away from it, that it wasn't safe to be around, just like the Indians who used to live on the Plains.

I daydreamed of a hundred thousand Indigenous heads like this one pushing up out of the land and water all around the globe, messengers, elders, the ancestors of all, causing everyone to pause for weeks and then months with their rumbling emergence; somehow like the opposite of a natural disaster. I contemplated this old Native in Seattle, felt grateful for him, wanted to figure out how to befriend him. His enormity was comforting to me, welcoming and protective.

I looked into his colorless eyes and felt one thousand percent sure—as Pike's Place Market surged almost right behind me—that he was looking back into mine.

GOOD CONTRACTS/GOOD CONTACTS

In this skin you hear the words
of the generation that's coming and
then the one behind them and the

one behind them too. You hear
them often enough and well enough
to get a sense of what you've got

to do to fashion things so that they
can have a decent chance at fulfilling
their destiny when they arrive.

It becomes an organizing river of
astral thought in your heart
and it connects you to so many

that the joy and beauty of it
almost always outshines the challenges
and responsibility that comes with it.

In this skin you hear like the
earth hears and at the end of
the day you wish such meaningful

sweetness and purpose on all.

CARRIED BY THE THUNDERBIRD

Sometimes I long for days
to know what my grandpa knew,
to have the watercolors of his
memories, the fireside stories
of his cultural knowledge inside
my own being.
It makes me sharp as a blade,
soft as grass, as awake as a
man being carried by a real-life
thunderbird-
it makes me into a quiet
warrior for our Ponca people's
towering spirit.
The longing to know what
my grandpa knew, or at least
a little something more of it,
carves and cleans me, funnels
me into a focused, hungry
dot.
He's not around anymore but
my thoughts of him keep delivering
me more gifts from him;
the longing I feel when I
think of him keeps me
in his company.

THEY PUT MY GRANDPA ON A STAMP

I reread a book about my grandpa Chief Standing Bear and feel every detail of his court case raindropping into me, falling from the great vivid sky of history into my finite mortal flesh. I want to disappear into the story, blossom out into its unfolding reality, reincarnate with tender, immortal strips of it in my contemporary form.

I pick up my phone and go on the post office's website to see how much they're selling the new Chief Standing Bear stamps for, to check them out. Can something the size of a postage stamp counteract any of the oceanic cultural loss we're living with? How many stamp-sized things does it take to make up for what was lost in your people's genocide?

Somewhere a teenager is receiving a monthly letter from their grandpa, and as they plop down on a couch crowded with books and a laptop and some blankets, looking for a moment at my proud and beautiful grandpa on the corner of the envelope, they surprise themselves with their sincerity when they ask aloud, "Who's that?"

GOLDEN MEDICINE ANTS

I walked past the iconic
Nebraska State Capitol all
alone, wrapped in the after
midnight silence.
To many, I had already fallen
through the cracks, been eaten
by the forces that dismantle
hope and promise, that make
people just disappear.
But inside me were bears hunting
delicious plants, buffalo that
were part of the earth's original
rumbling, inherited dreams that
dwarfed most modern things,
rivers capable of recarving
the landscape itself.
I was lonely but also humming
with a well-loved and cared-for
inner world, an internal cultural
organ that gave me so much
that I knew that I could never
give it away.
I kept going around the capitol
on my way home—
a golden medicine ant in the
singing shadow of the state's
mythical center.

PACKING A GOOD LUNCH

In a distant future that's somehow located just above our own, our ancestors are packing the medicine luggage for Ponca souls who're just about ready to jump into their new bodies and lives. Grandpas and grandmas are making sure they have all sorts of little things they're going to need for their purpose, their trials, their adventures, the transit of their traumas, their tight spots and unending joys. Uncles are layering strength into them, aunties are handing them humor, and old lovers are singing songs into them that they'll never forget and also on the surface immediately forget too. All for a distant time that I can barely conceive of, but that I can feel and that I can clear as day see them preparing for.

I stare up at them as people in downtown Astoria move around me on their way to all sorts of things that their ancestors tried their best to prepare them for, and wonder what life on earth would be like if everyone could see what I'm seeing, wonder what it would be like if everyone knew just how intimately involved our ancestors really are in our lives.

I keep looking up and imagine what the world looks like where they're going.

LESSONS FROM KEVIN

A little embarrassed, among the hundred
people dancing at the reception, I dance
with my sweetheart's dad getting my

much-needed lessons. "Push and then
pull, push and then pull," he says,
lit up and happy, exactly where he

wants to be somehow, leading me.
"Do you get it?" I kind of do,
but also kind of don't. "I think

I got it," I say, the only man
dancing with another man but who
cares. He releases me and I wander

over to my gorgeous partner in a
new cowgirl hat and a beautiful dress,
grab her and pull her towards me.

"Let's dance," I say, happy
myself and blissfully lost in wedding
joy, "but this time let me lead,

this time let the Ponca lead."

GUARDIANS OF THE TIME-STORM: PART ONE

Not even out of Middle School, I laid back on my bed in my tiny bedroom in the trailer in which we lived and I squirmed. My mom was asleep in the back bedroom (or at least pretending to be, to escape my dad), my dad was drinking and watching TV in the living room. I could sense his demons; the drinking brought them out like clockwork. I was sad, unsafe, an Indian kid very daily on the edge of breaking into two.

I began to drift around some, surrounded by my comic books, my sketchbooks, and then I was pulled back by a tap on my window. I blinked and zeroed in. Nobody had ever tapped on my trailer window in my life. But holy crap: I looked and saw a Chewbacca, a true Bigfoot filling up the window and looking in on me. My insides went tight. He looked like something that hadn't taken a human bath with soap and shampoo even once in his life. He also had something to him that made him as intoxicating to behold as some flowers that people only stumbled across maybe once every couple of decades.

I froze.

He talked to me with his mind. "Sneak out when your dad's going to the bathroom. I've got something to show you."

GUARDIANS OF THE TIME-STORM: PART TWO

A few minutes later, spellbound and excited with a weird, lively energy swirling inside of me, my dad went to the bathroom that shared a wall with my little bedroom and I grabbed my shoes and tiptoed through the living room, out the door and down the steps, right outside to where the big, imposing, rough-looking, and totally mystical Bigfoot was waiting for me. He stood there like the Conan-sized protector I'd always wished I'd had when my dad and his demons were cutting me up or beating on me. He looked friendly but serious.

"How fast can you run?" he asked me with his mind-talk.

"Fast enough," I said aloud, looking behind me where I was sure my dad was back in our living room.

"Then follow me!"

He took off running, leaping over the waist-high corrugated steel fence and into the farmer's old spooky corn. I didn't think twice: I went right after him, running behind him, in the backsplash of his energies, getting slapped by dry leaves, getting scraped up and scratched up good. But a kind of supernatural fun filled me to the brim. My feet were small and it was dark but somehow I kept up, somehow I stayed close enough to keep smelling him.

GUARDIANS OF THE TIME-STORM: PART THREE

We ran through the night and he mind-yelled 'Jump!' and we both jumped above the corn, into the air, through accelerating sheets of strange lights, beyond the sky, like two action figures slingshotted past the earth's atmosphere into another dimension where we were suddenly flying as natural as birds or butterflies. I zipped right behind him, then beside him, trying to orient myself. His large furry mass guided me, directed my body as I tried to grasp things with my mind.

"It'll only take a few minutes but I'm going to take you to your world's future-storm," he said. "The place where your earth's future is born. Whatever you don't understand, you'll get someday. Just listen, young Leatherback. That's what's most important."

We slipstreamed through indescribable rivers of light and sound, passing entry-points to other worlds, massive leviathans coasting and tunneling, herds of other beings I had no names for. We slipped, blurred, were invisible, then ultra-visible, were a tight, slick unit on a mission. The minutes warped me, made me more myself too. And then we were there.

"Behold, young Ponca, the birth center of your world's time."

GUARDIANS OF THE TIME-STORM: PART FOUR

He was right; it did look like some kind of chaotic, semi-spherical storm happening in a paradoxically loaded/empty space. I could feel the earth's soul all around us, flowing over us like waves of emotion from a galaxy-inhabiting, magnificent, ancient being. I wanted to close my eyes and dissolve completely into it.

"There's more here than what you're seeing," my Bigfoot guide said. "I've adjusted things so that you can perceive the main things, which are this: you have ancestors telling stories inside that bright time-storm and they're perpetually winning but never completely victorious because that part depends on a larger thing we're all working on. Different ancestors of yours go in there and come out. Some stay for a long time, some can only handle a short plunge. Because see, there are other forces in there too, strong, noisy, story-breakers. You make stories. They break stories. The making always wins. But the breaking always hurts. You're in the hurt part now but you're going to spend the rest of your life in the making."

He paused and we floated. The time-storm was silvery, snapping, exploding, a shifting world too large to see into, seething, cloaked, bursting, loud. We were pebbles to its ocean, grass to its mountain. I could feel the time pouring out of it into the plane of our world, shaping trillions of moments into pattern after pattern, story-wave after story-wave, fate and future after fate and future. My little mind trembled and comprehended what it could. Part of me wanted to cry, while another part of me wanted to sing along with all the Ponca songs I was hearing in the faraway distance.

"You can feel Mother Earth's soul, yes?"

I nodded.

"All the story-makers can. She's your guide."

He hung there in the light-stream, looking into the time-storm.

"There's so much more to say but in a minute we're going to have to go back."

I wobbled, tried to hold still.

"Mother Earth's mind is in there and there's a great story she's busy telling but these other forces want to cause us all to jump stories, to jump onto a different track, a story a being other than the earth is telling. It's a war in there, but it also isn't. Sometimes we're on the verge of losing, but we never really are. Other things besides Mother Earth's love want to rule, but they never really can. The people of Turtle Island are key to this all, the Poncas are key to this all. Mother Earth became land and the land became people and you are the luminous storytelling tip of that grand planetary process. You've got to express what's inside you so that Mother Earth's love can speak the truest future into being, so that this time-storm births everything just right. Is that as clear as the water of the Loup River on a perfect sunny day?"

He put his big hairy arm around me and held me, pulled me in a little close. I did not understand him at all; and yet maybe I did.

"Clear as the river," I said, and then I started falling backwards.

GUARDIANS OF THE TIME-STORM: PART FIVE

I woke up in the cornfield, his smell everywhere around me but no sight of him at all. It was still night. I walked back through the scratchy old corn, slow and buoyant, tired and fried.

When I got to our trailer I could hear that the TV was off, that my dad must've called it a night. I quietly snuck back in, tiptoed again through the trailer, slipped off my clothes and crawled into bed. I looked out my window and searched for the time-storm, for its unstable electric mass, and saw only moonlight, the brown trailer of our neighbor next door.

I was dead-tired and began to fall asleep. Did what just happened really just happen? Did I really just go on a spirit-mission with a Bigfoot to learn about and look at the thing that was actually birthing the future of our world? Did I really feel the waves of Mother Earth's soul on my little body? Was I really some sort of storyteller who was going to ensure that the right story won and became everyone's reality?

I took in a deep whiff of the Bigfoot's smell and decided that in time I'd know, maybe not tomorrow, maybe not even in a decade, but in time I'd know.

ROOM FOR ONE MORE

We touched the bottom of the water-bucket to the hot, glowing stones and then set it back down onto the ground. There were five of us in the lodge; me, my partner, my buddy who was about to walk across the country, a local elder, and a young Dine' beadworker. It was hot and we were already sweating, two-leggeds in the first womb, half-made prayer travelers in a lodge-ship with the bird-filled world and still earth heat-shimmering outside the door. I adjusted and looked at the rocks, felt the silence of the Other World seeping in around us, pervading the moment.

Then I was pulled out of my slowly-expanding reverie by a familiar voice, his giant furry fingers immediately seen in my periphery.

"Hey, nephew, is there room for one more?"

We all turned and looked at him, the hulking Bigfoot that if you hadn't already had the experience of meeting you'd at least heard about him from someone who had. His manifold strength flowed into our circle, his spirit filling the gaps around us as the others instinctively began scrunching together to make space for him. He was as ancient as the old-growth and as up-to-date as tomorrow's next TikTok sensation. I wasn't as spun by his appearance as I used to be.

I made a kind of joke, replying, "If you're here to pray then you can come on in, but if you're here to just tell your crazy stories then you better wait outside."

He looked at me and showed me his teeth.

"Okay," I said, looking back at the rocks, "come on in then."

HER FEATHERED SKIN

A hummingbird zips around and pauses
outside my kitchen window as I eat
my eggs and toast.

It changes colors, transmits the essence
of the Creator, pulses with subtle light,
opens portals into the realms

beneath Nature's skin, births little
words from its exquisite form that
travel into my chest.

I drink my coffee and feel the
faith that buds and branches and
turns at the center of our world,

looking up into the galactic layers of
encompassing compassionate life,
sure of how things will ultimately

shake out. The hummingbird digs
its needle-like beak into a pink flower
and drinks, illuminates all of Astoria,

touches me, letting me know that to
see a hummingbird in the morning is
to see a fantastic iridescent goddess

carrying on right in front of you.

CHIEF SMOKE MAKER

I sit with Standing Bear in a Niobrara hotel on the day when he expresses our portion of the tribe's desire to stay in our original homelands to the four committee men who've traveled to speak with us on behalf of President Hayes. I'm wearing modern cargo shorts and a long-sleeve blue-and-white flannel and I'm right beside Chief Smoke Maker, the oldest Ponca in the room. We are wrinkles and fur and pain and tempered hope. We're the land looking back at representatives of a people who've completely forgotten who they are, who are wrecking and twisting the earth's story into all the wrong directions.

Standing Bear, dressed in civilian clothes, walks up and down the floor, building protective walls, peeling monsters out of our midst, pushing his will towards the President, mourning the buffalo, advocating for a future that I, a hundred and forty some years later, am actually living. I breathe in the proceedings with my spirit, absorb his tribe-given geometries, send them forward through the generations, and basically experience it all in awe.

He meets eyes with his old friend and foe General Crook and says, "If the Great Father tried to give me a million dollars for my land, I would not take it. My children have been exterminated, my brother has been killed. I strive for what is good and that alone. I will not be scared, and I will not be driven into another bad hole."

He pauses and Smoke Maker turns to me, so many elders pouring through him that it almost knocks me out of what's unfolding. His face moves into mine, like a spiritual limb extending, and the river, the bluffs, his ancestors, the tough plants, all begin talking both into me and beyond me all at once.

I become a corridor in time through which Smoke Maker's medicine leaps and spirits through, more passageway than Ponca, more medicine tunnel than man. I warp and hold steady, break apart and stay present.

Standing Bear continues on and I get fierce, using all of my might to not fall away as Smoke Maker grows and sends his medicine and oldest prayers through me.

2012/RAISE A GLASS

I see Clark crossing the street
two blocks down on First Friday Artwalk
and wonder if maybe I should run
to catch up with him despite
how tired and out-of-it I feel.
He has a green water bottle in hand,
a shoulder bag full of some of the
earth's best writing (crafted by him
in obscurity over the years) and
assorted unimaginable magical objects
I'm sure.
He's like a centaur, an absinthe poet,
a Japanese shaman-priest, a late-night
Seattle dive-bar crooner—
man, am I lucky to have a brother
like him.
He heads up the block and I painfully
turn home, unable to enter into
the frenzy of Friday night, a chance
to hang with Clark vanishing with my
consent right in front of me.
I feel him stalking into the wolf party,
the bars, intentionally odd artists, Galaga
machines, readings, and howls,
and I swim for safety, aloneness,

sanctuary—
for a time when I'm strong enough
to party with the wolves like him.

RIDING THE BUFFALO INTO THE MOONRISE WITH ONLY ONE ARROW IN MY BACK AND WITH TWO BABIES CRADLED TO MY CHEST

I sink into my theater seat, munching on my second bucket of popcorn, and take in hour sixteen of Ponca director William Larvie's insane and insanely beautiful magnum opus Riding the Buffalo into the Moonrise with Only One Arrow in My Back and With Two Babies Cradled to My Chest. Amazingly, the theater is still mostly full.

I'm half a body and half a spirit following along through this wild flood of poetic Ponca stories that're depicting all eras of our tribal history (which he begins with a two hour cartoon animation of our Creation Story) and even several very realistically rendered eras of our future history. I'm on the back of a dragonfly, watching a pair of leathery hands make a bow; am inside a blind mother crawling from a tragic car accident; am in the joint with a trio of Poncas, knowing that only two will make it out, and only one will be intact and functional. These are the kinds of grand artistic expressions my young art-powered self from the nineties dreamed of for my people in that last century. The scale finally meets the depth of what wants to be told. My tribe gets to speak in a way that feels clear, total, unhindered—fully realized.

And there are still about 11 hours left. I've sat through this six times before, nodding off here and there throughout like most do. I'm so fucking glad that this is what it means to be a Native on Turtle Island today. And I pray the imagined future history at the end of this film is exactly the kind of comprehensively Indigenous-centered reality that ultimately comes to pass.

I slurp on my soda and watch a Ponca medicine man float over a steaming hill to rescue some imprisoned ghosts, and feel completely like I'm somehow right there too.

EXPLAINING THE SACRED
IN THE AIRPORT

My bag is flagged like it
always is and I take a deep

breath and explain to them that
I'm a Native person and I'm

going back to Nebraska for Sundance
and that that's my pipe in

the bag. They ask me to carefully
remove it and I do, never

feeling that great about having
to withdraw my bowl in the

noisy chaos of the airport but
accepting it and assuming the

spirits do too. They see that
I'm on the up and up and let

me go, rejoining Aislinn who's
putting her shoes and stuff back

on. I set my stuff down
and rush with the same myself,

glad to have gotten through the
whole experience one more time

again.

BACKYARD CEREMONIES

After the sweat we all had a big pot-luck in our backyard and everything tasted so delicious. We all ate too much, the kids were running around like ninjas, and the sea lions in the distance kept up with their yapping and music. I was tired, a little raw, but just so happy to be with so many friends and relatives that were all just so happy too (even if it was just for the time being).

I looked behind me and saw a world that I used to think only I could see, but now I was old enough to know that everyone else saw it too, just sort of in their own way.

I saw my ancestors, several Bigfoot with big medicine staffs, too many crazy little people to count, hawks, eagles, butterflies, floating rivers, mountain chunks, and trees older than time itself, among so many others, countless others who were all safeguarding our souls, our joy, and our future.

I laughed and tuned into my brother's conversation. Everything felt like it was about to get really interesting. Like I was the time-traveling Ponca and I'd finally found myself in front of the right medicine-carrying storyteller.

PART THREE

THEY HONOR OUR FAMILY

Up at Sundance in the sweat, I see a little person sitting on the rocks pouring out a can of Pepsi. It makes me chuckle. These little guys are always cracking me up, making sure my understanding of the sacred is just the right kind of serious and not too serious too.

My brother praying beside me is known worldwide (okay, Nebraska-wide) as a hardcore, lifelong Pepsi drinker. I figure they're joshing him, teasing him by pouring out some of his favorite cola onto the red-hot rocks. Oh, the humor of it all. But then, mind-melding with this little person, I remember that my Pepsi-loving friend's mom just passed two months ago—a grandma that deserves far more honoring than I have the space for here—and I suddenly comprehend that this spirit was being funny but now he's also being serious by pouring out some Pepsi to honor the passing of our beloved, we're-all-gonna-miss-her-to-our-last-day grandma. The grief hits me and I watch the little relative with a humble, solemn heart.

"The teaching here," he says, looking at me, "is that those who can laugh as big and beautifully as your brother here are only capable of doing so because of how deeply they can feel the sadness, pain, and grief of the people. How they laugh is connected to how deeply they're willing to feel the people's suffering."

I try to really hear what he's saying, his emptying out of the Pepsi can taking on a whole new light in the darkness. I pray for my brother. I pray for my grandma who is no longer among us.

THE LAST 30 YEARS

At the end of my long life I see
that there are more Native books,
movies, documentaries, comics, and
art in general, than any one

Native, even the most dedicated one,
could hope to read and see and
experience in their lifetime—
no matter how much they'd want to

there's just too much Native-made
stuff out there for them to ever
go through it all. And that's all
just happened in the last 30 YEARS.

Can you wrap your head around the
sheer immensity of what our collective
Native consciousness has delivered into
the body of our wild, hurting world?

Can you launch off from there and
imagine what that same collective
Native consciousness is going to do
in the next 30 years, the next century?

I pull the memoirs of a Pawnee
shaman professor down from my shelves
and get comfortable in my bed,

cough, drink my herbal tea, and

prepare to go on one more Indigenous
adventure that my younger self
was always, always dreaming of.

NATIVE POSTCARDS

Native postcards of all kinds, from all times, rain down from a white cloud outside my hometown.

They pile up, people take them, people burn them, the government gets involved, us Natives get involved—really it's a pretty spectacular thing.

The cloud stays for years and you start seeing those magical postcards everywhere; it's a kind of proof the world just accepts, the land herself telling everyone that us Natives know some things and that it's time for folks to start listening, to really hear us for the sake of our combined futures.

I visit the cloud as often as I can. I try to go when no one else is there. I sage myself off and walk out into the drizzle of fluttering cards, getting bonked and dinged, getting blessed by the civilization-altering phenomenon.

I close my eyes and wonder what it all means, wonder at it all, wonder myself right into the feelings I hope everyone one day has a lot more of.

STANDING BEAR IN LINCOLN

I pulled my luggage down the paths
of the Centennial Mall, tired from
so much more travel on such an already
long trip, emotionally ready to finally go

see the statue of Chief Standing Bear
they'd erected since I'd moved away.
I passed college kids with bags of fast
food, eyed the phallic capitol building,

and then slowed when I saw him
standing there, 20 feet tall, arm
outstretched, posing with something
beyond pride until the next person

came up to talk to him. This time,
the next person was me. I rolled my
stuff over to him and sat down, ran
my hand over his huge beaded moccasins,

admitted that I was at a mountain I'd
need more than one visit to fully
experience. I thought, if he'd been
here when I lived here I'd have been

happily visiting him everyday—I mean
how could I not. What if you were a
lonely invisible twentysomething Native

kid in the Midwest, a kid who's almost

been killed multiple times by different
manifestations of an uncaring culture, and there
was a colossal bronze statue of your Ponca Chief
grandpa just a few blocks away from

where you lived? What a thing it
would've been had he been here like this
all of those 14 years I lived in downtown
Lincoln. Our visits would've

been something else, our visits would've
been legend. I grabbed a water-damaged
copy of my newest book and got out a
pinch of tobacco and placed it all

at his feet, made a prayer as some
more college kids walked past me.
My grandpa never abandoned me. My
grandpa has always been there, guiding

me about how to be Ponca and how to
use my gifts to help our people.
I sank into a feeling-space that was
part of our shared soul and communed

with his radiant reality, our tribe's
Plains-made radiant reality, and
then I said fuck it to my ingrained
self-consciousness, and began to sing

a prayer song. And the singing felt
so good that I sang three more after
that, looking around in the altered
space, savoring the long-time-coming

visit, blending with Lincoln and my
grandpa and the past and the sacred
Other World that had brought me and
all of my luggage to this place in

the world. Sad the singing was done,
happy to be there. I had no doubts
about my work. Just like 50
years ago the spirits knew that there

was going to be a statue of Chief Standing
Bear there someday, I always knew
that I'd be telling my people's story
all across the land in ways that could never/

were impossible to disappear; in ways
that the deep genius of my tribe had
foreseen over a century ago; and I was
just the beginning. There was no one

around to witness this moment but
I was witnessing it and that made it
as real, as alchemically-potent as it
needed to be. I basked, I breathed,

I ached, I floated, and I felt

as much as I was able to feel. And then I got going. A Ponca rolling his luggage away from his immortal

Indian Chief grandpa. A Ponca alive with the immortal blessings of his people.

THE OFFICE (PONCA EDITION)

After my keynote I sit in the background
at the Ponca tribal offices eating delicious
leftovers and being happily quiet.
My cousin, my niece, new faces,
online friends, a white tech woman
with a mohawk, a brother just out of
prison—all who work for the tribe—
and more, eat and laugh and make
leftover boxes to take home and it's
all like some Ponca Tribe version of
The Office.
I can feel the unbreakable threads
of love and joy and pride that our
ancestors are weaving through our
modern lives, even here, maybe
especially here.
Where we go, they go, whether
we're offering tobacco up in Niobrara
or watching our kid's soccer game
in Lincoln; like the braids in
our hair and the lights in our eyes,
they are with us.
I mix my beef tips with my mashed
potatoes and chomp them down, laugh
when everyone else laughs, try to follow
along with their casual Friday office talk.

I'm an old Ponca that some of them
have known since I was a kid, making
a cameo in this episode of their show
and I feel blessed.

INFINITE PRAYERS

Prayer ties on Bear Butte that don't
disintegrate.
Surrounding towns empty and then disappear,
cell towers fall, cars are swallowed.
But Bear Butte remains wrapped in
prayer ties like some old Mayan pyramid
wrapped protectively by the jungle.
Eons pass.
Space-faring beings from other galaxies
descend to investigate.
They're giants, half biological, half
machine.
They behold Bear Butte, see
the ties.
The prayers in the ties bring them
deferentially to what would be one
of their knees.
They can see the glow of the people's
world draped around the being of the
butte.
They depart.
Wind blows over the land, ringing
the ties ever so slightly.
The prayers of the people continue on,
more infinite than anything else
our vanished species had ever
made.

YOUTH FORESHADOWING ADULTHOOD

I enthusiastically collected baseball cards
when I was a kid, then I rabidly
collected comics as an adolescent,
and now I collect Indian knowledge

like my people's future depends on it,
which it kind of does. I'm old enough
now to realize that the spirits had me
practicing in my youth for what I was

to spend my whole adult life doing
once I got old enough—and in fact
my youth in its entirety, was constructed
along those future-considering lines

in general. Dear reader, dear relative,
dear fellow Indigenous Futurist: maybe
yours was too. We don't come here to
waste our gifts. The hells of our childhoods

have secret magic hidden in them. Our
purpose was setting up shop long before we
knew its name. The cartoon we watched
was preparing us to be an arborist. My

youth was foreshadowing the medicine work
of my adulthood. Maybe yours was too.

THE STORYTELLING DESCENDANTS

Three futuristic young Natives sitting around a fire with bits of technology silently floating around their heads. One has a tattoo that almost imperceptibly moves across their face, like a strange shadow. Another is thin but palpably heavy with the amount of traditional knowledge they carry. And the last has a braid thicker than an arm hanging down their front.

"That 500 years where we were almost edged out is important to remember," the one with the braid says. "The stain of it is still in our bones and you can feel it if you try hard enough. It's there."

The thin one gazes into the fire, listens to one of those technology bits, then says, "The planet was suffering because we weren't following the Original Instructions she gave us. We were a lost species then, killing more and more the more lost we became."

The tattooed one goes somewhere within themselves and then comes back. "A relative a thousand years ago is writing about us right now," they say, reflecting and then smiling. "From the tail end of that time, right before our Indigenous wisdom began DJing the whole big dance party again."

The tattooed one looks at me again and then says, "We're surrounded by a thousand years of revitalized Medicine and those sensitive ones way back there can feel its deep reality and presence in the storytelling of their bones too."

GRANDPA TAYLOR'S HOUSE

A dream where I'm showing up early, very
early at my grandpa Taylor's house
the day of someone's funeral. It's an Indian
house and there're about 15 or so people all
sleeping in the living room, passed out on the
couch, in chairs, all over the floor, wherever
there's an inch of space, including my dad
who's wearing a white pocket tshirt like my
grandpa always used to wear. They all
kind of wake up, sleepily coming back to life,
and I worry that they're waking because of me but
then realize they were going to be waking up soon
anyway. I don't know who the funeral's for.
To my right I see some elders, cousins of
my grandpa with almost stone faces who
I've never met; they make me feel a
bit like a kid, relieved because they're
the keepers of the light and it means I don't
have to be present as the central keeper
myself. Did I mention what a complete
warm hug it feels like to be with my Indian
family? Surrounded, encompassed, held, an
integral part of a big Soul that I can feel,
that extends beyond my perception's reach.
I'm on the couch beside an Inuit guy who's
come down for the funeral and he's telling me

the story of this guy from his tribe who
cooked up this whole story about why he had
to 'resign' or exile himself from his people,
like his people were a job he could quit from.
It's a load of hogwash, the Inuit is telling me;
totally. I distill what he's saying and reflect it
back, saying, The land knows the truth of all
this world's bullshit. Exactly, he says, nodding
his head. It's the worst circumstances to have to
come back for but it feels good to be back home.
I look at my grandpa's cousins and they're just
about the only ones fully dressed, ready to do
what must be done. I relax and I rise at the same
time, circled with love but knowing that I'm here
to help with what needs to happen too.

NO PHONE, NO BOOKS

Lying on the ground by the fire
in the middle of the night,
wet from the mist, pretty tired,

but dedicated to the point of
something like paranoia to keeping it
going for the person who's fasting.

No phones here, no books, only
animals in the dark, birds,
paper hole-punched moon, and the

fire that is both alive and as
consistently psychedelic as anything
I've ever seen. I unwrap myself, half

sit up and reach over for another
piece of wood, expertly add it
to the fire. Here I'm in a zone

where what is untouched by the slimy
hands of civilization comes forward and
begins to tell me stories I've wanted

to hear my whole life. Here I step
outside of time and tend things like
the prayer-man I've always known

myself to really be.

JUPITER'S BOOKS

Simple times.
You've got to be kidding me!
I asked if I was supposed to be
there, looked down, and found
a thunderstone.
Appalachian seven generations back
on both my father's and mother's
side.
They asked me to speak and
I remembered Puck's line from
Shakespeare's A Midsummer Night's Dream.
Shakespeare was just a dude like
the rest of us.
What she said hit the power-chord
of my heart.
Everything collapsed and at the end
I was like a salmon who'd done all
that he could and wound up not
making it, flopping on the shore.
How do you say 'thank you'
in Ponca?
I said, man, you're a goddamned
trickster!
We've got to take care of the ponies
of our soul no matter how bad
it gets.

People just kept coming into
the bookshop telling me the latest
news.
When I get going I know how
people see me: they see me as
so much bad theater.
That whale offered herself up
onto the shore for a reason and
we cannot forget her in all
of this.
As good as it all gets, sometimes
you gotta step outside and just
listen to the crickets.
The light-switches had little
signs on them that said, *Please
be good stewards and turn off
the lights when you leave.*
I want to go back to those high
bluffs overlooking the Niobrara
when I realized I was in Ponca Country.
It's a lost cause but at least
we're still two brothers making
medicine.
In her people's language, she
said, When the time's right you'll
find a way to give him that blanket.
The Indigenous People need
to be in the driver's seat!
Yes, those little people are real—

they've got shoes, cooking utensils,
musical instruments, and everything!
The canoe was called The Dragonfly
and its carver was standing right there.
That elder in Wounded Knee said,
That's a Medicine Gathering song.
The cedar trees talk too.
What about Creation?
She said she was afraid of spiders
and was ashamed of it, and I said,
You probably have a spider sensitivity
because you're meant to work with
them somehow, so you shouldn't
feel any shame at all.
I'm grateful for everything, even
the sunlight on that water
over there.

OCEAN PLANS

I came out of Before Sunset in a
romantic's aching daze, wandering
through the dark campus, asking

life when I'd finally find someone
to walk through Paris with and
fall into beautiful, imperfect love

with. Twenty years later I wake
up beside someone who's life's
reply to that long ago question;

my sweetheart I walk through Astoria
with, and I'm more in love with
her with each passing year.

We stayed in bed for 45 minutes
after she got up, didn't have
breakfast together, made plans to

go to the ocean today, probably
will, probably will even kiss
innumerable times as the enormous

ocean lets us know that she's
always happy to see us.

THEY STILL CRY

I wake up to a developing news story
about the Genoa Indian School,
the boarding school that was about
20 miles from my hometown.

It looks like they've used ground
penetrating radar to locate the 'lost'
cemetery and have found approximately
80 children's bodies.

What kind of schools were these?
They were the kinds of schools where
dozens if not hundreds of Indian kids
died at them, were buried, forgotten,

never got to go home again. I stare
out the window and wish I could
go back in time to rescue those
kids, destroy that school, make

sure that zero kids died there.
I would've gathered up all those schools
and beaten them all into the ground,
bloodied and broken my knuckles so that

all of those Indian kids could run home
and be free.

THE GIFT OF OUR WORDS

Our words travel to the young, even to the unborn. Down the road they'll wear clothes we can't picture, have hobbies not invented yet, have homes riddled with technology none of us can imagine; but our words will be with them, like inherited medicine plants and wildflowers carpeting the backyards of their souls.

Words that pulse, that walk through walls, that know about the stars, that guide with smells, that taste better than anything that's been touched by a machine, that drip health, that swim with the old names, that crackle with lightning, that know how to stir up knowing, that create connection to the longed for, that're beauty incarnate.

We've got to fill up the world, time, and the night with all of our most heartfelt and gorgeous and unforgettable storytelling and prayers and words that we've got, because they're going to be born with our words living inside of the caverns and waters and lands of them, but we want to make sure they're getting born with the most beautiful renditions of the words of any who've ever lived.

This is what my words tell me.

And to my great joy, I really see it happening.

JUST AN OLD DREAM

I imagine how far off into the future
Poncas will still be receiving dreams
from the Niobrara, from our old homelands,

and am visited by the sturdiest of joys.
The timeless real world is there like
the ground beneath our feet, in the actual

land beneath our feet; not a step of
anyone's journey would be possible without
Her there every moment of the way.

I was there just a few weeks ago,
Her dreams filtering through me, remaking
me, chiseling my stone into the shape

of an Old Ponca like all the ones
never discovered, never removed, who're
still all out in the sunlight of Her

lands. Her dreams made me. I'm just
an old dream of the land where the
Niobrara empties into the Missouri River

and as far as I'm concerned that's
the best dream I could ever hope
to be.

AUNT DEBBIE

My great Aunt Debbie comes to the Sundance. I try to give my dad fair warning. He quickly gathers up his stuff where we're all sitting by our tent, even putting on his shoes but not tying them up, and runs/clomps/scurries over to his tent, positioning himself directly behind ours so that he's out of eyesight from where we're at. He has his reasons, haha.

Debbie comes over with her walker, is helped to sit down by Aislinn and me and then, after she gets comfortable with her water and everything else, she looks up and behind her without really moving her head and says, "Junior! Are you afraid of me? Why the hell are you hiding back there?!"

My dad, found out, yells back, like a smiling kid caught, "I'm not. I'm doing something back here."

"Well, you better get over here when you're done."

A few minutes later he comes back with all of his stuff, 66 years old and sheepish, his shoes still untied.

"I'm telling Little Cliff stories," she says, "and you better sit down and listen to them too because as you can see by looking at me, I'm not going to be around here forever."

He sits down, we all chuckle (maybe even a little uneasily), and the once-in-a-lifetime storytelling begins.

DISMANTLED LANCES

All the way into my thirties, having
never left Nebraska, I was afraid
of people seeing me. The lance pierced

through so many generations: what could
happen to you on the Plains/in the Midwest
if your real identity as a lightning-carrying

spiritual Indigenous person was publicly
witnessed; and who was there to protect you,
especially in these times? Low-profile.

Invisibility. Erasure. Execution. Then I
left, Standing Rock happened, community
healed me, I decided to quit hiding;

I and the culture changed simultaneously. It
became time to dismantle the lance, show
others that it could be done, illustrate

how we can free up the generations so that they
have a better chance than we did. I'm a bit
wild now, but bravery and responsibilities require

it. I was on a track to hide myself my whole
life but thank the ancestors I was freed
from that suffering. Thank the ancestors

I can now write my books, sweat in my

backyard, challenge this damn creature-
feature we're in, and luminously be

myself.

THE 12,000 YEAR OLD INDIAN

Joe was a medicine man so I really listened to the things he had to say, really absorbed as many of his stories as I could.

I was down in New Mexico doing some things, he said, and I was heading towards this mountain to meet up with some friends.

I was by myself, cruising along, when I saw this old Indian walking on the shoulder of the road. Just old looking. Quiet. It was so hot out I got kind of worried about him immediately. So I pulled over ahead of him and stopped the car.

He walked up and I asked him what he was doing.

He said, I'm heading up to that mountain to collect some medicine.

I asked him if he needed a ride. He said sure, he'd take a ride.

So, he got in and we got going and eventually we got to talking. Very strangely, he said he knew who I was, said he'd seen me before. I got a good memory and knew I'd never seen him before, but he was sure, without arguing, he was sure.

I kept looking at his face out of the corner of my eye: it was like leather, lots of lines, a kind of shine to it. He started telling me the history of where we were, of the tribes there, but of things far, far back in their memory, in their history.

He was talking like a spirit and the vibe in the car changed. I just kept driving, kept listening.

He asked me about my work and I told him I was a spiritual man for my people and he said that's what he was too. I told him a little about my ceremonies and he said that he was familiar with those ceremonies, that that's most certainly where he'd seen me.

Then he started telling me about his ceremonies, the work he did with the mountains, the underground waters and caverns, the things under cities, the plants and birds and old people who knew about him that he liked to visit. Much of it was all stuff I'd never heard of before. I tried to remember what he was saying, his points, his reasoning, his stories.

Then, he said, I'm 12,000 years old. Do you believe that? We were passing a gas station, a kid was working on his bike. I shivered. I nodded. I said, Yeah, I do, grandpa. Then he started telling me about his life, why and how he was alive so long, what being alive so long allowed him to do for the land and the people. It was pretty unbelievable. He told me miracle stories, about the beings he worked with, the way he understood everything that was unfolding in time here in the Western Hemisphere. He told me about some of his doctoring ceremonies, what he carried in his heart for the future of all life on our planet. I listened, and I drove. Must've been in that car together for a little over an hour and a half, but it felt like more. Then, kind of randomly, he said, Can you let me out here? I pulled over. We shook hands. And then he went walking off into a field, sort of disappearing, and sort of not, and then I just got going and drove away.

When I met up with my friends on the mountain later—some of whom were Indian doctors down there—I told them a little bit about the old man I'd picked up, who said he needed a ride to the mountain, and they all looked at one another and said they knew him. Well, none of them had ever seen him but they'd heard stories of him catching rides to the mountain going back to the beginnings of cars themselves. They said he'd been around, as far as they knew, as long as he said he'd been. He was a force down there, and they respected him. They had met elders who'd talked to him and who he'd pass things along to here and there.

I've seen him a few other times, Joe said. Never like I did down in New Mexico, but in my ceremonies, he's come to a couple of my ceremonies. When I call the spirits, he's shown up, given me medicine or advised me on how to proceed.

Why I'm telling you this, Joe said, is because some of the things I've told you over the years came from this 12,000 year old man and I want you know to that. Some of the teachings now living in you come from him. And now you know a bit of his story, enough to contribute to any talk of him if he ever comes up with anyone in your lifetime, enough to maybe even recognize him if you ever encounter him yourself.

Forces like him, Joe said, are in our midst all the time.

Even when we're not thinking about them, he said, they're there.

RIVERS IN YOUR CLOTHES

Rivers in your clothes.
Ancestors in your teeth.
The Great Past working
through you to make
the Great Future.
The fire, the soil,
the hair of your lover.
The way a prayer
touches the one praying.
Being Ponca until the
end of time.
People covered in plants
and flowers again, like
they'd been caught in
a magical rain.
Death faced with
drum in hand.
Like old friends
together again.
The sparkle in a
Bigfoot's eyes.
The oldest story
freshly alive in you.
Beauty weeping with joy
throughout your life.
The earth waking up again
in sweet, perfect silence.